Born in 1984
by
Kerry Butters.

Born in 1984.

Millennium: 2nd millennium

Centuries: 19th century – **20th century** – 21st century

Decades: 1950s 1960s 1970s – **1980s** – 1990s 2000s 2010s

Years: 1981 1982 1983 – **1984** – 1985 1986 1987

1984 (MCMLXXXIV) was a leap year starting on Sunday (dominical letter AG) of the Gregorian calendar, the 1984th year of the Common Era (CE) and *Anno Domini* (AD) designations, the 984th year of the 2nd millennium, the 84th year of the 20th century, and the 5th year of the 1980s decade.

Contents

Events

January

- January 1
  - Brunei becomes a fully independent state.
  - Bell System in the United States is broken up.
- January 3 – President of the United States Ronald Reagan meets with Navy Lieutenant Robert Goodman and the Reverend Jesse Jackson at the White House, following Lieutenant Goodman's release from Syrian captivity.
- January 5 – President Ronald Reagan nominates Elizabeth Dole as U.S. Secretary of Transportation.
- January 7 – Brunei becomes the sixth member of the Association of Southeast Asian Nations (ASEAN).
- January 10
  - The United States and the Vatican (Holy See) restore full diplomatic relations.
  - The Victoria Agreement is signed.

- January 18 – The Mitsui Miike coal mine explosion at Ōmuta, Fukuoka, Japan, kills 83.
- January 22 – The national release of the iconic 1984 advertisement
- January 24 – Apple Computer places the Macintosh personal computer on sale in the United States.

February

- February 1 – Medicare comes into effect in Australia.
- February 3
  - Dr. John Buster and the research team at Harbor–UCLA Medical Center announce history's first embryo transfer from one woman to another, resulting in a live birth.
  - STS-41-B: Space Shuttle *Challenger* is launched on the 10th Space Shuttle mission.
- February 7 – Astronauts Bruce McCandless II and Robert L. Stewart make the first untethered space walk.
- February 8–19 – The 1984 Winter Olympics are held in Sarajevo, Socialist Federal Republic of Yugoslavia.
- February 13 – Konstantin Chernenko succeeds the late Yuri Andropov as General Secretary of the Communist Party of the Soviet Union.
- February 26 – The United States Marine Corps pulls out of Beirut, Lebanon.
- February 29 – Canadian prime minister, Pierre Trudeau, announces his retirement.

March

- March 5 – Iran accuses Iraq of using chemical weapons; the United Nations condemns their use on March 30.
- March 6 – A year-long strike action begins in the British coal industry (see UK miners' strike (1984–85)).
- March 14 – Sinn Féin's Gerry Adams and three others are seriously injured in a gun attack by the Ulster Volunteer Force.
- March 16 – The United States Central Intelligence Agency station chief in Beirut, William Francis Buckley, is kidnapped by the Islamic Jihad Organization and later dies in captivity.
- March 22 – Teachers at the McMartin Preschool in Manhattan Beach, California are charged with Satanic ritual abuse of the school children; the charges are later dropped as completely unfounded.
- March 23 – General Rahimuddin Khan becomes the first man in Pakistan's history to rule over two of its provinces, after becoming interim Governor of Sindh.
- March 25
  - Pope John Paul II consecrates the world to the Immaculate Heart of Mary, in Fátima, Portugal.
  - The Institute of the Incarnate Word (IVE) is founded under Fr. Carlos Miguel Buela.

April

Diretas Já demonstration held in São Paulo.

- April 1 – Marvin Gaye is shot to death by his father, one day before his 45th birthday.
- April 2 – Indian Squadron Leader Rakesh Sharma is launched into space, aboard the *Soyuz T-11*.
- April 4 – U.S. President Ronald Reagan calls for an international ban on chemical weapons.
- April 9 – The 56th Academy Awards, hosted by Johnny Carson, are held at the Dorothy Chandler Pavilion. *Terms of Endearment* wins Best Picture and 4 other Academy Awards.
- April 12 – Palestinian gunmen take Israeli bus number 300 hostage. Israeli special forces storm the bus, freeing the hostages (one hostage, two hijackers killed).
- April 13 – India launches Operation Meghdoot, bringing most of the disputed Siachen Glacier region of Kashmir under Indian control and triggering the Siachen conflict with Pakistan.
- April 15
    - English comedian Tommy Cooper suffers a massive heart attack and dies while live on TV.
    - The first World Youth Day gathering is held in Rome, Italy.

- April 16 – More than one million people, led by Tancredo Neves, occupy the streets of São Paulo to demand direct presidential elections during the Brazilian military government of João Figueiredo. It is the largest protest during the Diretas Já civil unrest, as well as the largest public demonstration in the history of Brazil. The elections are granted in 1989.
- April 17 – WPC Yvonne Fletcher is shot and killed by a secluded gunman, leading to a police siege of the Libyan Embassy in London.
- April 19 – "Advance Australia Fair" is proclaimed as Australia's national anthem, and green and gold as the national colours.
- April 23 – United States researchers announce their discovery of the AIDS virus.
- April 24 – An X-class solar flare erupts on the Sun.
- April 25 – The term of Sultan Ahmad Shah as the seventh Yang di-Pertuan Agong of Malaysia ends.
- April 26 – Sultan Iskandar of Johor, becomes the eighth Yang di-Pertuan Agong of Malaysia.

May

- May 2 – The International Garden Festival opens in Liverpool.
- May 5 – The Herreys win the Eurovision Song Contest 1984 for Sweden, with the song "Diggi-Loo, Diggi-Ley".
- May 8
  - The Soviet Union announces that it will boycott the 1984 Summer Olympics in Los Angeles.

- - Denis Lortie kills three government employees in the National Assembly of Quebec building.
  - The Chicago White Sox defeat the Milwaukee Brewers 7-6 in the longest game in Major League Baseball history: 25 innings totalling eight hours, six minutes.
- May 11 – A transit of Earth from Mars takes place.
- May 12 – The Louisiana World Exposition, also known as the 1984 World's Fair, and also the New Orleans World's Fair, and, to the locals, simply as "The Fair" or "Expo 84", opens.
- May 13 – An explosion at the Soviets' Severomorsk Naval Base destroys two-thirds of all the missiles stockpiled for the Soviets' Northern Fleet. The blast also destroys workshops needed to maintain the missiles as well as hundreds of technicians. Western military experts called it the worst naval disaster the Soviet Navy has suffered since WWII.
- May 14 – The one dollar coin is introduced in Australia.
- May 17 – Michael Silka kills nine people near Manley Hot Springs, Alaska.
- May 19 – The Edmonton Oilers win The Stanley Cup, beating the defending champion New York Islanders in 4 games to 1.
- May 23 – A methane gas explosion at Abbeystead water treatment works in Lancashire, England, kills 16 people.
- May 27 – An overnight flash flood rages through neighborhoods in Tulsa, Oklahoma. Nearly 15 inches of rain falls in some areas over a four-hour period; 14 people are killed.
- May 31 – Six inmates, including James and Linwood Briley, escape from a death row facility at Mecklenburg

Correctional Center, the only occasion this has ever happened in the United States.

June

- June 1 – William M. Gibbons is released as receiver and trustee of the Chicago, Rock Island & Pacific railroad, after all of its debts and creditors are paid off by order of a federal bankruptcy court.
- June 3 – Ronald Reagan visits his ancestral home in Ballyporeen, the Republic of Ireland.
- June 4 – Bruce Springsteen release's his 7th album Born in the U.S.A.
- June 5 – The Indian government begins Operation Blue Star, the planned attack on the Golden Temple in Amritsar.
- June 8
  - A deadly F5 tornado nearly destroys the town of Barneveld, Wisconsin, killing nine people, injuring nearly 200, and causing over $25,000,000 in damage.
  - Ghostbusters is released.
- June 12 – In one of the greatest NBA Finals ever, The Boston Celtics beat the Los Angeles Lakers in 7 games to capture their 15th NBA Championship.
- June 16 – The world-renowned, critically acclaimed Canadian entertainment company, Cirque du Soleil is founded.
- June 18 – Colorado radio host Alan Berg is shot dead outside his home in Denver by members of The Order.

- June 20 – The biggest exam shake-up in the British education system in over 10 years is announced, with O-level and CSE exams to be replaced by a new exam, the GCSE.
- June 22
  - The official name of the Turkish city of Urfa is changed into Şanlıurfa.
  - Virgin Atlantic Airways makes its inaugural flight.
- June 27 – France beats Spain 2–0 to win Euro 84.
- June 28 – Richard Ramírez (the "Night Stalker") murders his first confirmed victim.
- June 30 – John Turner becomes Canada's 17th prime minister.
- June 30 – Elton John plays the famous Night and Day Concert at Wembley Stadium.

July

- July 1 – Liechtenstein becomes the last country in Europe to grant women the right to vote.
- July 13 – Terry Wallis, a 19-year-old living in the Ozark Mountains of Arkansas, falls into a deep coma after a severe automobile accident (he will eventually awaken 19 years later on June 13, 2003).
- July 14 – New Zealand Prime Minister Rob Muldoon calls a snap election and is heavily defeated by opposition Labour leader David Lange.
- July 18
  - Beverly Burns becomes the first woman Boeing 747 captain in the world.

- In San Ysidro, San Diego, 41-year-old James Oliver Huberty sprays a McDonald's restaurant with gunfire, killing 21 people before being shot and killed himself.

Newspaper vending machine featuring news of the 1984 Summer Olympics, which opened on July 28.

- July 23 – Vanessa L. Williams becomes the first Miss America to resign when she surrenders her crown, after nude photos of her appear in *Penthouse* magazine.
- July 25 – *Salyut 7*: cosmonaut Svetlana Savitskaya becomes the first woman to perform a space walk.
- July 28–August 12 – The 1984 Summer Olympics are held in Los Angeles, California.

August

- August 1 – Australian banks are deregulated.
- August 4 – The African republic Upper Volta changes its name to Burkina Faso.
- August 4 – Soviet submarine *K-278 Komsomolets* reaches a record submergence depth of 1,020 meters.
- August 11
  - United States President Ronald Reagan, during a voice check for a radio broadcast remarks, "My fellow

Americans, I'm pleased to tell you today that I've signed legislation that will outlaw Russia forever. We begin bombing in five minutes".
  - Barefoot South African runner Zola Budd, controversially granted British citizenship earlier in the year, collides with Mary Decker of the U.S. in the Olympic 3000 meters final, neither finishing as medallists.
- August 16 – John DeLorean is acquitted of all eight charges of possessing and distributing cocaine.
- August 17 – Peru recognizes the Sahrawi Arab Democratic Republic.
- August 21 – Half a million people in Manila demonstrate against the regime of Ferdinand Marcos.

The launch of shuttle, *Discovery*, on STS-41-D, its first mission.

- August 30 – *STS-41-D*: the Space Shuttle *Discovery* takes off on its maiden voyage.

September

- September 2 – Seven people are shot and killed and 12 wounded in the Milperra massacre, a shootout between the rival motorcycle gangs Bandidos and Comancheros in Sydney, Australia.
- September 4
  - The Progressive Conservative Party of Canada, led by Brian Mulroney, wins 211 seats in the Canadian House of Commons, forming the largest majority government in Canadian history.
  - The long running British children's TV show *Thomas & Friends* debuts on ITV.
  - The Sandinista Front wins the Nicaraguan general elections.
- September 5
  - *STS-41-D*: the Space Shuttle *Discovery* lands after its maiden voyage at Edwards Air Force Base in California.
  - Western Australia becomes the last Australian state to abolish capital punishment.
- September 10 – *Jeopardy!* begins its syndicated version.
- September 14 – P. W. Botha is inaugurated as the first executive State President of South Africa.
- September 16 – Edgar Reitz's film series *Heimat* begins release in Germany.
- September 17 – Brian Mulroney is sworn in as Prime Minister of Canada.
- September 18 – Joe Kittinger becomes the first person to cross the Atlantic, solo, in a hot air balloon.

- September 20 – Hezbollah car-bombs the U.S. Embassy annex in Beirut, killing 24 people.
- September 23 – The television drama *Threads*, a documentary of nuclear war, broadcasts on BBC Two.
- September 26 – The United Kingdom and the People's Republic of China sign the initial agreement to return Hong Kong to China in 1997.

October

- October 4 – Tim Macartney-Snape and Greg Mortimer become the first Australians to summit Mount Everest.
- October 5 – *STS-41-G*: Marc Garneau becomes the first Canadian in space, aboard the Space Shuttle *Challenger*.
- October 11 – Aboard the Space Shuttle *Challenger*, astronaut Kathryn D. Sullivan becomes the first American woman to perform a space walk.
- October 12 – The Provisional Irish Republican Army (PIRA) attempts to assassinate Prime Minister Margaret Thatcher and the British Cabinet in the Brighton hotel bombing.
- October 19 – Polish secret police kidnap Jerzy Popiełuszko, a Catholic priest who supports the Solidarity movement. His dead body is found in a reservoir 11 days later on October 30.
- October 23 – The world learns from moving BBC News television reports presented by Michael Buerk of the famine in Ethiopia, where thousands of people have already died of starvation due to a famine, and as many as 10,000,000 more lives are at risk.

- October 25 – The European Economic Community makes £1.8 million available to help combat the famine in Ethiopia.
- October 31 – Assassination of Indira Gandhi: Prime Minister of India Indira Gandhi is assassinated by her two Sikh security guards in New Delhi. Anti-Sikh riots break out, leaving 10,000 to 20,000 Sikhs dead in Delhi and surrounding areas with majority populations of Hindus. Rajiv Gandhi becomes Prime Minister of India.

November

- November 6 – United States presidential election, 1984: Ronald Reagan defeats Walter F. Mondale with 59% of the popular vote, the highest since Richard Nixon's 61% popular vote victory in 1972. Reagan carries 49 states in the electoral college; Mondale wins only his home state of Minnesota by a mere 3,761 vote margin and the District of Columbia.

Presidential election results map. Red denotes states won by Reagan/Bush (49), Blue denotes those won by Mondale/Ferraro (1+D.C.).

- November 9 – Cesar Chavez delivers his speech, "What The Future Holds For Farm Workers And Hispanics", at the Commonwealth Club in San Francisco.

- November 11 – The Louisiana World Exposition, also known as The 1984 World's Fair, and also the New Orleans World's Fair, and, to the locals, simply as "The Fair" or "Expo 84", closes.
- November 14 – Zamboanga City mayor Cesar Climaco, a prominent critic of the government of Philippine President Ferdinand Marcos, is assassinated in his home city.
- November 19 – A series of explosions at the Pemex Petroleum Storage Facility at San Juan Ixhuatepec, in Mexico City, ignites a major fire and kills about 500 people.
- November 25
    - An East Rail train derails between Sheung Shui and Fanling stations, Hong Kong.
    - Band Aid (assembled by Bob Geldof) records the charity single "Do They Know It's Christmas?" in London to raise money to combat the famine in Ethiopia. It is released on December 3.
    - Uruguayan presidential election, 1984: Julio María Sanguinetti is democratically elected President of Uruguay after 12 years of military dictatorship.
- November 28 – Over 250 years after their deaths, William Penn and his wife Hannah Callowhill Penn are made Honorary Citizens of the United States.
- November 30 – The Tamil Tigers begin the purge of the Sinhalese people from North and East Sri Lanka; 127 are killed.

December

Controlled Impact Demonstration

- December – A peace agreement between Kenya and Somalia is signed in the Egyptian capital Cairo. With this agreement, in which Somalia officially renounces its historical territorial claims, relations between the two countries began to improve.
- December 1 – Controlled Impact Demonstration: NASA and the FAA crashes a remote controlled Boeing 720.
- December 2 – Bob Hawke's government is re-elected in Australia with a reduced majority.
- December 3
  - Bhopal disaster: A methyl isocyanate leak from a Union Carbide pesticide plant in Bhopal, Madhya Pradesh, India, kills more than 8,000 people outright and injures over half a million (with more later dying from their injuries the death toll reaches 23,000+) in the worst industrial disaster in history.
  - British Telecom is privatised.
- December 4
  - Sri Lankan Civil War: Sri Lankan Army soldiers kill 107-150 civilians in Mannar.
  - Hezbollah militants hijack a Kuwait Airlines plane and kill 4 passengers.

- December 8 – White supremacist and Order leader Robert Jay Mathews is killed in a gun battle and fire during an FBI siege on Whidbey Island.
- December 10 – Cisco Systems is founded.
- December 14 – Nigeria recognizes the Sahrawi Arab Democratic Republic.
- December 19 – The People's Republic of China and United Kingdom sign the Sino-British Joint Declaration on the future of Hong Kong.
- December 22
    - Four African-American youths (Barry Allen, Troy Canty, James Ramseur, and Darrell Cabey) board an express train in the Bronx borough of New York City. They attempt to rob Bernhard Goetz, who shoots them. The event starts a national debate about urban crime in the United States.
    - In Malta, Prime Minister Dom Mintoff resigns.
- December 28 – A Soviet cruise missile plunges into Inarinjärvi lake in Finnish Lapland. Finnish authorities announce the fact in public on January 3, 1985.

Date unknown

- 1983–85 famine in Ethiopia intensifies with renewed drought by mid-year, killing a million people by the end of this year.
- Crack cocaine, a smokeable form of the drug, is first introduced into Los Angeles and soon spreads across the United States in what becomes known as the crack epidemic.
- The Chrysler Corporation introduces the first vehicles to be officially labeled as "minivans". They are branded as the

Chrysler Town & Country, Dodge Caravan, and Plymouth Voyager.

Births

January

Calvin Harris

Arjen Robben

Kid Cudi

- January 1 – Michael Witt, Australian rugby league player
- January 2 – Kristen Hager, Canadian film and television actress
- January 6 – Kate McKinnon, American actress, voice actress, and comedian
- January 7 – Max Riemelt, German actor
- January 8
  - Jeff Francoeur, American baseball player
  - Steven Kanumba, Tanzanian actor and director (d. 2012)
- January 10 – Marouane Chamakh, Moroccan football player
- January 12 – Scott Olsen, American baseball player
- January 13
  - Eleni Ioannou, Greek martial artist (d. 2004)
  - Nathaniel Motte, American songwriter, performer, singer, music producer, film composer, instrumentalist, and playwright (3OH!3)
- January 15
  - Megan Quann, American swimmer
  - Victor Rasuk, American actor
- January 16 – Craig Beattie, Scottish footballer
- January 17
  - Sophie Dee, Welsh pornographic actress
  - Cassie Hager, American basketball player
  - Calvin Harris, Scottish singer-songwriter
- January 18
  - Seung-Hui Cho, Korean-born American Virginia Tech massacre gunman (d. 2007)
  - Makoto Hasebe, Japanese footballer
- January 19

- o Thomas Vanek, Austrian hockey player
- o Trent Cutler, Australian rugby league player
- o Zakia Mrisho Mohamed, Tanzanian long distance runner
- January 20
  - o Olivia Hallinan, English actress
  - o Toni Gonzaga, Filipina actress, singer, and TV host
- January 21 – Richard Gutierrez, Filipino actor
- January 22 – Raica Oliveira, Brazilian supermodel
- January 23 – Arjen Robben, Dutch footballer
- January 24 – Witold Kiełtyka, Polish musician (d. 2007)
- January 25
  - o Robinho, Brazilian footballer
  - o Stefan Kießling, German football player
  - o Kaiji Tang, American voice actor
- January 26 – Luo Xuejuan, Chinese swimmer
- January 27 – Davetta Sherwood, American actress and musician
- January 28 – Andre Iguodala, American basketball player
- January 29
  - o Nuno Morais, Portuguese footballer
  - o Natalie du Toit, South African swimmer
- January 30
  - o Chad Power, American actor
  - o Kid Cudi, American hip hop artist
  - o Xi Zhang, Chinese contemporary artist

February

Carlos Tevez

Aubrey O'Day

Beren Saat

Cam Ward

- February 1
  - Lee Thompson Young, American actor (d. 2013)

- o Darren Fletcher, Scottish football player
- February 3 – Kim Joon, South Korean rapper, actor, and model
- February 4 – Mauricio Pinilla, Chilean footballer
- February 5
  - o Nate Salley, American football player
  - o Carlos Tevez, Argentinian football player
- February 6 – Darren Bent, English footballer
- February 9
  - o Han Geng, Chinese singer in Korea (Super Junior)
  - o Logan Bartholomew, American actor
- February 10 – Kim Hyo-jin, Korean actress
- February 11 – Aubrey O'Day, American singer and actress
- February 12
  - o Jennie McAlpine, English television actress and comedian
  - o Brad Keselowski, American stock car driver
- February 13 – Brina Palencia, American voice actress
- February 14 – Robbie Jones, American television and film actor
- February 15 – Dorota Rabczewska, Polish singer and model
- February 16
  - o Oussama Mellouli, Tunisian swimmer
  - o Fábio Lucindo, Brazilian voice actor
- February 17 – AB de Villiers, South African cricketer
- February 18 – Genelle Williams, Canadian actress
- February 19 – Marissa Meyer, American novelist
- February 20 – Ben Lovejoy, American hockey player
- February 21
  - o Karina, Japanese model and actress

- o Damien Molony, Irish television actor
- February 22 – Tommy Bowe, Irish rugby union footballer
- February 25
  - o Filip Šebo, Slovak footballer
  - o Xing Huina, Chinese athlete
- February 26
  - o Beren Saat, Turkish actress
  - o Emmanuel Adebayor, Togolese footballer
- February 28 – Karolína Kurková, Czech model
- February 29
  - o Alicia Hollowell, American softball pitcher
  - o Cullen Jones, American swimmer
  - o Cam Ward, Canadian hockey player

March

Olivia Wilde

Justine Ezarik

Fernando Torres

- March 1
  - Claudio Bieler, Argentinian football player
  - Naima Mora, American winner of *America's Next Top Model*, cycle 4
  - Brandon Stanton, American photographer and blogger
- March 2 – Ian Sinclair, American voice actor
- March 3 – Hayley Marie Norman, American actress and model
- March 4
  - Tamir Cohen, Israeli footballer
  - Ai Iwamura, Japanese actress

- o Zak Whitbread, American soccer player
- o Whitney Port, American television personality, clothing designer, and author
- March 7
  - o Brandon T. Jackson, American stand-up comedian, actor and rapper
  - o Mathieu Flamini, French football player
- March 8
  - o Ross Taylor, New Zealand cricketer
  - o Nora-Jane Noone, Irish actress
- March 9 – Julia Mancuso, U.S. Olympic medalist
- March 10 – Olivia Wilde, American actress
- March 12 – Jaimie Alexander, American actress
- March 16
  - o Michael Ennis, Australian rugby league player
  - o Hosea Gear, New Zealand Rugby Union player
- March 19 – Bianca Balti, Italian model
- March 20
  - o Fernando Torres, Spanish football player
  - o Nomura Yuka, Japanese actress
  - o Christy Carlson Romano, American stage and film actress
  - o Justine Ezarik, Internet celeberity and actress
- March 21
  - o Kerry Bishé, American model, actress and reality television star
  - o Sopho Gelovani, Georgian singer
- March 24
  - o Chris Bosh, American basketball player
  - o Park Bom, Korean singer

- March 25 – Katharine McPhee, American Idol finalist
- March 26
  - Stéphanie Lapointe, Canadian singer
  - Sara Jean Underwood, American model
- March 28 – Nikki Sanderson, English actress
- March 30
  - Anna Nalick, American singer
  - Samantha Stosur, Australian tennis player
  - Justin Moore, American country music singer

April

Mandy Moore

Nikola Karabatić

America Ferrera

Aram Mp3

- April 1 – Murali Vijay, Indian cricketer
- April 2 – Shawn Roberts, Canadian actor
- April 3 – Allana Slater, Australian gymnast
- April 4 – Sean May, American basketball player
- April 5 – Saba Qamar, Pakistani actress and model
  - Marshall Allman, American actor
  - Aram Mp3, Armenian singer-songwriter, comedian and showman.
  - Phil Wickham, Contemporary Christian vocalist, songwriter and guitarist
- April 8 – Kirsten Storms, American actress
- April 9

- o Adam Loewen, Canadian pitcher
- o Linda Chung, Canadian TVB actress and singer
- April 10
  - o Mandy Moore, American singer and actress
  - o Cara DeLizia, American actress
  - o Natasha Melnick, American television and film actress
- April 11
  - o Kelli Garner, American actress
  - o Nikola Karabatić, French handball player
- April 12 – Emmy, Armenian singer
- April 13
  - o Kris Britt, Australian cricketer
  - o Hiro Mizushima, Japanese actor and writer
- April 14 – Kyle Coetzer, Scottish cricketer
- April 16
  - o Amelia Atwater-Rhodes, American author
  - o Claire Foy, English actress
- April 17 – Rosanna Davison, Irish model, Miss World 2003
- April 18
  - o Red Bryant, American football player
  - o America Ferrera, American actress
- April 19 – Lee Da-hae, South Korean actress
- April 20
  - o John Jairo Castillo, Colombian football player
  - o Tyson Griffin, American MMA fighter
  - o Nelson Évora, Portuguese athlete
- April 22
  - o Michelle Ryan, English actress
  - o Amelle Berrabah, British singer (Sugababes)
- April 23 – Alexandra Kosteniuk, Russian chess player

- April 24 – Tyson Ritter, American singer/songwriter (The All-American Rejects)
- April 25 – Melonie Diaz, American actress
- April 26 – Brett Novek, American male fashion model and actor
- April 27 – Patrick Stump, American singer (Fall Out Boy)
- April 29
  - Taylor Cole, American actress and model
  - Kirby Cote, Canadian Paralympic swimmer
  - Firass Dirani, Australian actor
  - Paulius Jankūnas, Lithuanian basketball player
  - Lina Krasnoroutskaya, Russian tennis player and commentator
  - Pham Van Quyen, Vietnamese footballer
  - Vassilis Xanthopoulos, Greek basketball player

May

Mark Zuckerberg

Kostas Martakis

Carmelo Anthony

- May 1
  - Alexander Farnerud, Swedish footballer
  - Keiichiro Koyama, Japanese singer (NEWS) and actor
  - Kerry Bishé, American actress
- May 3 – Cheryl Burke, American professional dancer
- May 4 – Little Boots, English pop singer
- May 7 – Alex Smith, American football player
- May 8 – Martin Compston, Scottish actor and former professional footballer
- May 9
  - Ezra Klein, American journalist, blogger and columnist
  - Prince Fielder, American baseball player
- May 11 – Andrés Iniesta, Spanish footballer

- May 12 – Junie Browning, American MMA fighter
- May 14
  - Michael Rensing, German footballer
  - Mark Zuckerberg, American founder and CEO of Facebook
  - Gary Ablett Jr., Australian rules footballer
  - Olly Murs, English singer and TV presenter
- May 15 – Samantha Noble, Australian actress
- May 17
  - Andreas Kofler, Austrian ski jumper
  - Passenger, English singer and songwriter
  - Christine Robinson, Canadian water polo player
- May 20
  - Dilara Kazimova, Azerbaijani singer and actress
  - Naturi Naughton, American singer and actress
- May 21 – Jackson Pearce, American novelist
- May 23 – Adam Wylie, American child actor
- May 24 – Sarah Hagan, American actress
- May 25
  - Unnur Birna Vilhjálmsdóttir, "Miss Iceland", crowned Miss World in 2005
  - Kyle Brodziak, Canadian ice hockey player
  - Emma Marrone, Italian pop/rock singer
  - Kostas Martakis, Greek singer, model and occasional actor
  - Nikolai Pokotylo, Russian singer
  - Marion Raven, Norwegian singer-songwriter, former child actress
- May 27 – Darin Brooks, American actor
- May 29

- Kaycee Stroh, American actress
- Carmelo Anthony, African-American basketball player
- May 31
  - Jason Smith, Australian actor
  - Milorad Čavić, Serbian swimmer
  - Yael Grobglas, Israeli actress

June

ByeAlex

Rick Nash

Paul Dano

Aubrey Plaza

Khloé Kardashian

- June 1
    - Olivier Tielemans, Dutch race-car driver
    - Naidangiin Tüvshinbayar, Mongolian judoka
    - Taylor Handley, American actor
- June 4
    - Rainie Yang, Taiwanese singer
    - Jillian Murray, American actress
- June 5 – Iris van Herpen, Dutch fashion designer
- June 6 – ByeAlex, Hungarian indie-pop singer and writer
- June 7 – Ari Koivunen, Finnish singer
- June 8
    - Todd Boeckman, American football player
    - Andrea Casiraghi, Prince of Monaco

- o Javier Mascherano, Argentinian footballer
- o Torrey DeVitto, American actress and former fashion model
- June 9 – Wesley Sneijder, Dutch footballer
- June 11 – Vágner Love, Brazilian footballer
- June 13 – Bérengère Schuh, French archer
- June 14 – Yury Prilukov, Russian swimmer
- June 15 – Tim Lincecum, American baseball player
- June 16
  - o Rick Nash, Canadian hockey player
  - o Emiri Miyasaka, Japanese model
- June 17 – John Gallagher Jr., American actor, singer and dancer
- June 19 – Paul Dano, American actor and producer
- June 23 – Duffy, Welsh singer
- June 24
  - o J. J. Redick, American basketball player
  - o Lucien Dodge, American voice actor
- June 25
  - o Lauren Bush-Lauren, American model
  - o Indigo (actress), American television and voice actress
  - o Killian Donnelly, Irish stage actor
- June 26
  - o Raymond Felton, American basketball player
  - o Deron Williams, American basketball player
  - o Lauren Harris, British vocalist
  - o Aubrey Plaza, American actress
- June 27
  - o Emma Lahana, New Zealand actress
  - o Khloé Kardashian, Television personality

- June 29 – Chris Egan, Australian actor
- June 30 – Fantasia Barrino, African-American singer

July

Rachael Taylor

Ali Krieger

- July 1 – Donald Thomas, Bahamian high jumper
- July 2 – Vanessa Lee Chester, American television and film actress
- July 3
  - Corey Sevier, Canadian actor
  - Syed Rasel, Bangladeshi cricketer
  - Manny Lawson, American football player
- July 4 – Jin Akanishi, Japanese singer (KAT-TUN and LANDS) and actor

- July 5 – Danay García, Cuban film actress
- July 6
  - Lauren Harris, English singer
  - D. Woods, American R&B singer, dancer, and actress
- July 7 – Mohammad Ashraful, Bangladeshi cricketer
- July 9
  - LA Tenorio, Filipino professional basketball player
  - Hanna R. Hall, American actress
  - Caroline D'Amore, American model, and actress
- July 11
  - Tanith Belbin, Canadian figure skater
  - Joe Pavelski, American hockey player
  - Rachael Taylor, Australian actress
- July 12
  - Gareth Gates, English singer
  - Amanda Hocking, American fantasy novelist
  - Michael McGovern, Northern Irish footballer
- July 16 – Katrina Kaif, Indian actress and model
- July 17 – Asami Kimura, Japanese singer
- July 18
  - Lee Barnard, English footballer
  - Liv Boeree, English poker player and TV presenter
  - Josh Harding, Canadian hockey player
- July 19
  - Lasse Gjertsen, Norwegian videographer
  - Diana Mocanu, Romanian swimmer
  - Alessandra De Rossi, Italian-Filipina actress
  - Andrea Libman, Canadian Actress, Voice Actress, Singer
- July 21

- o Paul Davis, American basketball player
  - o Iris Strubegger, Austrian model
- July 23
  - o Brandon Roy, American National Basketball Association player
  - o Celeste Thorson, Asian American actress, model
- July 24 – Tyler Kyte, Canadian actor/singer
- July 26 – Kyriakos Ioannou, Cypriot high jumper
- July 27
  - o Antoine Bethea, American football player
  - o Taylor Schilling, American actress
- July 28
  - o Ali Krieger, American soccer player
  - o Zach Parise, American hockey player
- July 29 – Todd Bosley, American actor
- July 30
  - o Anna Bessonova, Ukrainian rhythmic gymnast
  - o Gabrielle Christian, American actress

August

Ryan Lochte

Quinton Aaron

Ann Hsu

Kenan Sofuoğlu

- August 1 – Bastian Schweinsteiger, German football player
- August 2 – Brandon Browner, American NFL player
- August 3
  - Carah Faye Charnow, American singer (Shiny Toy Guns)
  - Ryan Lochte, American swimmer

- Kyle Schmid, Canadian actor
- August 5 – Helene Fischer, German singer and entertainer
- August 6 – Marco Airosa, Angolan footballer
- August 7 – Ann Hsu, Taiwanese actress and model
- August 10 – Ryan Eggold, American film and television actor
- August 11 – Melky Cabrera, American Major League Baseball outfielder for the Kansas City Royals
- August 12
  - Yua Aida, Japanese model and pornographic actress
  - Sherone Simpson, Jamaican athlete
- August 13 – James Morrison, English singer/songwriter and guitarist
- August 14
  - Clay Buchholz, American Major League Baseball pitcher
  - Robin Söderling, Swedish tennis player
- August 15 – Quinton Aaron, American actor
- August 17 – Garrett Wolfe, American NFL player
- August 19
  - Micah Alberti, American model and actor
  - Simon Bird, English actor and comedian
- August 20
  - Mirai Moriyama, Japanese actor
  - Tsokye Karchung, Bhutanese beauty queen, Miss Bhutan 2008
- August 21
  - Alizée Jacotey, French singer
  - Melissa Schuman, American singer and actress
- August 22 – Lee Camp, English footballer

- August 23 – Glen Johnson, English footballer
- August 24
    - Kyle Schmid, Canadian actor
    - Charlie Villanueva, American basketball player
    - Yesung, Korean singer (Super Junior)
- August 25 – Kenan Sofuoğlu, Turkish professional motorcycle racer
- August 27 – Josh Duhon, American actor
- August 28
    - Him Law, Hong Kong actor
    - Sarah Roemer, American model and actress
- August 31
    - Ryan Kesler, American ice hockey player
    - Charl Schwartzel, South African golfer

September

Garrett Hedlund

Prince Harry

Katie Melua

Laura Vandervoort

Avril Lavigne

- September 1 – Joe Trohman, American singer-songwriter, composer, and guitarist (Fall Out Boy)
- September 2 – Danson Tang, Taiwanese actor, model, and singer
- September 3 – Garrett Hedlund, American actor
- September 6
  - Maksymenko Igor Volodymorovych, Ukrainian kickboxer
  - Orsi Kocsis, Hungarian model
- September 7
  - Farveez Maharoof, Sri Lankan cricketer
  - Vera Zvonareva, Russian tennis player
  - Kate Lang Johnson, American actress and model
- September 10 – Luke Treadaway, English actor
- September 12 – September, Swedish singer and songwriter
- September 14
  - Adam Lamberg, American actor
  - Ayushmann Khurrana, Indian actor

- September 15 – Prince Harry, British Prince and son of Charles, Prince of Wales and Diana, Princess of Wales
- September 16
  - Sabrina Bryan, American actress and singer
  - Katie Melua, Georgian-English singer
  - Ali Fedotowsky, American television personality
- September 18
  - Jack Carpenter, American actor
  - Dizzee Rascal, English rapper
- September 19 – Kevin Zegers, Canadian actor
- September 20
  - Brian Joubert, French figure skater
  - Holly Weber, American actress and model
- September 21 – Dwayne Bowe, American football player
- September 22
  - Theresa Fu, Hong Kong singer and actress
  - Laura Vandervoort, Canadian actress
- September 23
  - Anneliese van der Pol, Dutch-born actress
  - Gabrielle Christian, American television and film actress and model
  - Kate French, American television and film actress and model
- September 25
  - Rashad McCants, American National Basketball Association player
  - Annabelle Wallis, English actress
  - Zach Woods, American actor and comedian
- September 26 – Keisha Buchanan, British singer (Sugababes)
- September 27

- ○ Avril Lavigne, Canadian singer
- ○ Abhinav Shukla, Indian actor
- September 28
  - ○ Melody Thornton, American singer (Pussycat Dolls)
  - ○ Helen Oyeyemi, British novelist
- September 29 – Per Mertesacker, German football player

October

Yoon Eun-hye

Lena Katina

Lindsey Vonn

Katy Perry

- October 1
  - Matt Cain, American baseball player
  - Mónica Spear, Venezuelan actress, Miss Venezuela 2004 (d. 2014)
- October 2
  - John Morris, American actor
  - Marion Bartoli, French professional tennis player
- October 3
  - Chris Marquette, American actor
  - Ashlee Simpson, American singer and actress
  - Anthony Le Tallec, French footballer

- o Yoon Eun-hye, Korean singer, model, actress and entertainer
  - o Laura Weissbecker, French actress
  - o Jessica Parker Kennedy, Canadian actress
- October 4
  - o Lena Katina, Russian singer (t.A.T.u)
  - o Álvaro Parente, Portuguese racing driver
- October 5 – Glenn McMillan, Brazilian-Australian actor
- October 6
  - o Joanna Pacitti, American singer
  - o Magdalena Frackowiak, Polish model
- October 7 – Ikuta Toma, Japanese drama actor
- October 10
  - o Chiaki Kuriyama, Japanese actress
  - o Steve Turner, Australian rugby league player
- October 12 – Emmanuel Kipchirchir Mutai, Kenyan long-distance runner
- October 13 – Kathrin Fricke, German web- and video-artist, known as Coldmirror
- October 14 – Santino Quaranta, American soccer player
- October 15 – Chris Olivero, American actor
- October 16
  - o Ben Smith, Australian rugby league player
  - o Shayne Ward, British singer
- October 17
  - o Chris Lowell, American actor
  - o Randall Munroe, American programmer and webcomic artist
- October 18
  - o Hollie Dunaway, American female boxer

- o Lindsey Vonn, American alpine skier
- October 19 – Kaio de Almeida, Brazilian swimmer
- October 21 – Marvin Mitchell, American football player
- October 23
  - o Izabel Goulart, Brazilian model
  - o Meghan McCain, American author and daughter of Senator John McCain
- October 24 – Emily Barclay, English-born New Zealand AFI award-winning actress
- October 25
  - o Sara Lumholdt, Swedish singer
  - o Katy Perry, American singer and actress
- October 26 – Sasha Cohen, American figure skater
- October 27
  - o Kelly Osbourne, English singer
  - o Brady Quinn, American football player
  - o Irfan Pathan, Indian cricketer
- October 28 – Obafemi Martins, Nigerian footballer
- October 29 – Eric Staal, Canadian hockey player
- October 30 – Eva Marcille, American model
- October 31
  - o Scott Clifton, American actor and singer
  - o Pat Murray, American football player
  - o Amanda Pascoe, Australian swimmer
  - o Nicole Rash, American model

November

Anastasia Karpova

Jena Malone

Scarlett Johansson

Marija Šerifović

Sanna Nielsen

Marc-André Fleury

- November 1
  - Miloš Krasić, Serbian footballer
  - Natalia Tena, English actress and singer
- November 2

- o Anastasia Karpova, Russian singer (Serebro)
- o Julia Stegner, German model
- o Tamara Hope, Canadian actress and singer
- November 3
  - o Christian Bakkerud, Danish race car driver (d. 2011)
  - o Ryo Nishikido, Japanese singer-songwriter and actor (NEWS and Kanjani Eight)
- November 4
  - o Dustin Brown, American hockey player
  - o French Montana, Moroccan-American rapper
  - o Ayila Yussuf, Nigerian footballer
- November 5
  - o Jon Cornish, Canadian football player
  - o Tobias Enström, Swedish ice hockey player
  - o Nick Folk, American football player
  - o Baruto Kaito, Estonian sumo wrestler
  - o Nick Tandy, English race car driver
  - o Nikolay Zherdev, Ukrainian-Russian ice hockey player
- November 6
  - o Ricky Romero, American baseball player
  - o Sebastian Schachten, German footballer
- November 7
  - o Amelia Vega, Miss Universe 2003, from the Dominican Republic
  - o Mihkel Aksalu, Estonian footballer
  - o Jonathan Bornstein, American soccer player
- November 8
  - o Steven Webb, English actor
  - o Kuntal Chandra, Bangladeshi cricketer (d. 2012)
- November 9

- o Beatrice Bofia, Cameroonian-American basketball player
  - o Delta Goodrem, Australian actress and singer
  - o Ku Hye-sun, South Korean actress and singer
  - o Joel Zumaya, American baseball player
- November 10
  - o Britt Irvin, Canadian actress and singer
  - o Jean-Martial Kipré, Ivorian footballer
  - o Jarno Mattila, Finnish footballer
  - o Ludovic Obraniak, Polish footballer
  - o Kendrick Perkins, American basketball player
- November 11
  - o Stephen Hunt, English footballer
  - o Birkir Már Sævarsson, Icelandic footballer
- November 12
  - o Omarion, American singer-songwriter and actor
  - o Sandara Park, South Korean singer (2NE1) and model
  - o Yan Zi, Chinese tennis player
- November 14 – Marija Šerifović, Serbian singer, Eurovision Song Contest 2007 winner
- November 17 – Park Han-byul, South Korean actress
- November 18 – Johnny Christ, American bassist (Avenged Sevenfold)
- November 19 – Lindsay Ellingson, American model
- November 21
  - o Lindsey Haun, American actress
  - o Jena Malone, American actress
- November 22 – Scarlett Johansson, American actress
- November 23 – Jarah Mariano, American model
- November 24

- o Ku Hye-sun, South Korean actress
- o Maria Riesch, German alpine skier
- November 25
  - o Ian Lacey, Australian rugby league player
  - o Gaspard Ulliel, French actor
- November 27 – Sanna Nielsen, Swedish pop singer
- November 28
  - o Andrew Bogut, Australian basketball player
  - o Marc-André Fleury, Canadian hockey player
  - o Trey Songz, African-American singer-songwriter, rapper, record producer, and actor
  - o Mary Elizabeth Winstead, American actress
- November 30 – Alan Hutton, Scottish professional footballer

December

Jackson Rathbone

Theo James

Basshunter

LeBron James

- December 4
    - Lauren London, American actress and model
    - Lindsay Felton, American actress
- December 7 – Robert Kubica, Polish Formula One racing driver
- December 8
    - Jennifer Grassman, American recording artist and journalist
    - Sam Hunt, American singer-songwriter
- December 11 – Xosha Roquemore, American actress
- December 12 – Daniel Agger, Danish football (soccer) player
- December 13 – Santi Cazorla, Spanish football player

- December 14
  - Chris Brunt, Northern Irish footballer
  - Jackson Rathbone, American actor and singer
- December 15
  - Yu Fengtong, Chinese speed skater
  - Martin Škrtel, Slovakian footballer
- December 16 – Laura More (Muncey), British singer
- December 16 – Theo James, English-American actor and singer.
- December 17
  - Asuka Fukuda, Japanese singer
  - Shannon Woodward, American actress
  - Tennessee Thomas, British-born American drummer and actor
- December 18
  - Julia Holter, American singer, songwriter and instrumentalist
  - Tiffany Mulheron, Scottish actress
- December 20 – David Tavaré, Spanish singer
- December 22 – Basshunter, Swedish DJ, Eurodance/Techno singer and record producer
- December 23
  - Alison Sudol, American singer-songwriter and pianist (aka A Fine Frenzy)
  - Cary Williams, American football player
- December 25
  - Jessica Origliasso, Australian singer-songwriter, actress and fashion designer
  - Lisa Origliasso, Australian singer-songwriter, actress and fashion designer

- December 26 – Jennifer Sipes, American actress and model
- December 27
  - Tye'sha Fluker, American basketball player
  - Rocío Guirao Díaz, Argentinian model
- December 28
  - Martin Kaymer, German golfer
  - Festus, American professional wrestler
- December 30 – LeBron James, African-American basketball player

Date Unknown

-
  - Mariko Ebralidze, Georgian jazz singer

Deaths

January

Johnny Weissmuller

- January 1 – Alexis Korner, British blues musician and broadcaster (b. 1928)
- January 6 – Ernest Laszlo, Hungarian-American cinematographer (b. 1898)
- January 7 – Alfred Kastler, French physicist, Nobel Prize laureate (b. 1902)
- January 9 – Sir Deighton Lisle Ward, Governor-General of Barbados (b. 1909)
- January 11 – Jack La Rue, American actor (b. 1902)
- January 13 – Ray Moore, American comic writer (b. 1905)
- January 14
  - Brooks Atkinson, American theater critic (b. 1894)
  - Ray Kroc, American entrepreneur (b. 1902)
  - Saad Haddad, Lebanese military officer and militia leader (b. 1936)
- January 17 – George Rigaud, Argentinian actor (b. 1905)
- January 20 – Johnny Weissmuller, Austrian-born swimmer and actor (b. 1904)
- January 21 – Jackie Wilson, American singer (b. 1934)
- January 22 – Sir Count Michael Gonzi, Archbishop of Malta and past politician (b. 1885)
- January 29 – Frances Goodrich, American screenwriter (b. 1890)
- January 30 – Luke Kelly, Lead Singer of Irish band The Dubliners (b. 1940)

February

Yuri Andropov

- February 8 – Karel Miljon, Dutch boxer (b. 1903)
- February 9 – Yuri Andropov, General Secretary of the Communist Party of the Soviet Union (b. 1914)
- February 10 – David Von Erich, American professional wrestler (b. 1958)
- February 11 – John Comer, English actor (b. 1924)
- February 12
  - Anna Anderson, Pretender to the Russian throne (b. 1896)
  - Julio Cortázar, Argentine writer (b. 1914)
- February 13 – Naomi Uemura, Japanese adventurer (b. 1941)
- February 15 – Ethel Merman, American singer and actress (b. 1908)
- February 21 – Mikhail Sholokhov, Russian writer, Nobel Prize laureate (b. 1905)
- February 22
  - Jessamyn West, American writer. (b. 1902)
  - Syed Faiz-ul Hassan Shah a Pakistani religious leader,of Allo Mahar Shrif. (b. 1911)

March

William Powell

- March 1 – Jackie Coogan, American actor (b. 1914)
- March 5
    - Tito Gobbi, Italian operatic baritone (b. 1913)
    - William Powell, American actor (b. 1892)
- March 6 – Henry Wilcoxon, British actor (b. 1905)
- March 10 – June Marlowe, American actress (b. 1903)
- March 12 – Arnold Ridley, English playwright and actor (b. 1896)
- March 16 – John Hoagland, American photographer (b. 1947)
- March 18
    - Charley Lau, American baseball player (b. 1933)
    - Paul Francis Webster, American lyricist (b. 1907)
- March 20 – Stan Coveleski, American baseball player (Cleveland Indians) and a member of the MLB Hall of Fame (b. 1889)
- March 23 – Shauna Grant, American pornographic actress (b. 1963)
- March 24 – Sam Jaffe, American actor (b. 1891)

- March 26 – Ahmed Sékou Touré, president of Guinea (b. 1922)
- March 31 – Jack Howarth, English actor (b. 1896)

April

Marvin Gaye

Arthur "Bomber" Harris

- April 1
    - Douglas Cooper, British art historian, critic and collector (b. 1911)
    - Marvin Gaye, American singer (b. 1939)
    - George Glass, American film producer and publicist (b. 1910)
    - Elizabeth Goudge, English writer (b. 1900)
- April 5
    - Arthur "Bomber" Harris, British air marshall (b. 1892)

- Giuseppe Tucci, Italian scholar of oriental cultures, (b. 1894)
- April 8 – Pyotr Kapitsa, Russian physicist, Nobel Prize laureate (b. 1894)
- April 9 – Willem Sandberg, Dutch typographer (b. 1897)
- April 11 – Edgar V. Saks, Estonian statesman and historian (b. 1910)
- April 15
  - Alexander Trocchi, Scottish writer (b. 1925)
  - Machito, Cuban singer and musician (b. 1908)
  - Tommy Cooper, Welsh comedian and magician (b. 1921)
- April 16 – Byron Haskin, American film and television director (b. 1899)
- April 17 – Mark W. Clark, American general (b. 1896)
- April 20
  - Hristo Prodanov, Bulgarian mountaineer (b. 1943)
  - Mabel Mercer, English cabaret singer (b. 1900)
- April 21 – Marcel Janco, Romanian-Israeli artist (b. 1895)
- April 22 – Ansel Adams, American photographer (b. 1902)
- April 23
  - Roland Penrose, English artist, historian and poet (b. 1900)
  - Vicente Solano Lima, Argentinian journalist and politician (b. 1901)
- April 24 – Rafael Pérez y Pérez, Spanish writer (b. 1891)
- April 25 – David A. Kennedy, son of Robert F. Kennedy (b. 1955)
- April 26

- Count Basie, American musician and composer (b. 1904)
- May McAvoy, American actress (b. 1899)
- April 30 – Rodrigo Lara Bonilla, Colombian lawyer and politician (b. 1946)

May

Diana Dors

John Betjeman

- May 2
  - Irwin Shaw, American author (b. 1913) Jack Barry, American television host and producer (b. 1918)
  - Bob Clampett, American cartoonist (b. 1913)
- May 4 – Diana Dors, English actress (b. 1931)
- May 6 – Mary Cain, Mississippi newspaper editor and politician (b. 1904)
- May 8 – Lila Wallace, American publisher (b. 1889)
- May 16

- ○ Andy Kaufman, American comedian (b. 1949)
- ○ Irwin Shaw, American author (b. 1913)
- May 19 – John Betjeman, English poet (b. 1906)
- May 21
  - ○ Andrea Leeds, American actress (b. 1914)
  - ○ Ann Little, American actress (b. 1891)
- May 22 – John Marley, American actor (b. 1907)
- May 24 – Vincent J. McMahon, professional wrestling promoter WWF (b. 1914)
- May 27 – Vasilije Mokranjac, Serbian composer (b. 1923)
- May 28 – Eric Morecambe, British comedian (b. 1926)

June

- June 2 – Fernando Zóbel, Filipino painter (b. 1924)
- June 6 – Jarnail Singh Bhindranwale, Sikh theologian, Most powerful Sikh leader of the 20th century (b. 1947)
- June 11 – Enrico Berlinguer, General Secretary of the Italian Communist Party (b. 1922)
- June 13 – António Variações, Portuguese singer (b. 1944)
- June 15
  - ○ Ned Glass, American actor (b. 1906)
  - ○ Meredith Willson, American composer (b. 1902)
- June 16 – Robert Mandrou, French historian (b. 1921)
- June 17 – Chet Allen, American actor (b. 1939)
- June 18 – Alan Berg, American talk radio host (murdered) (b. 1934)
- June 19 – Lee Krasner, American painter (b. 1908)
- June 20 – Estelle Winwood, English actress (b. 1883)
- June 22 – Joseph Losey, American film director (b. 1909)

- June 24 – William Keighley, American film director (b. 1889)
- June 25 – Michel Foucault, French philosopher (b. 1926)
- June 26 – Carl Foreman, American screenwriter (b. 1914)
- June 28
  - Yigael Yadin, Israeli archeologist, politician and Military Chief of Staff (b. 1917)
  - Claude Chevalley, French mathematician (b. 1909)
- June 30
  - Henri Fabre, pioneer French aviator & inventor (b. 1882)
  - Lillian Hellman, American playwright (b. 1905)

July

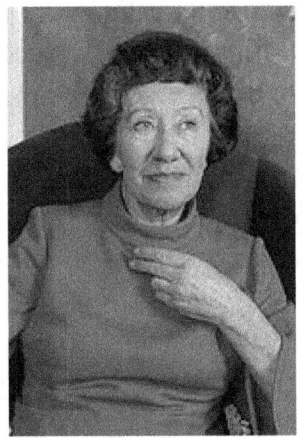

Flora Robson

George Gallup

James Mason

- July 1 – Moshé Feldenkrais, Ukrainian founder of the Feldenkrais Method (b. 1904)
- July 4 – Jimmie Spheeris, American singer-songwriter (b. 1949)
- July 7 – Flora Robson, English actress (b. 1902)
- July 8 – Brassaï, Hungarian-born photographer (b. 1899)
- July 14 – Philippé Wynne, American musician (b. 1941)
- July 17 – Karl Wolff, German Nazi SS Officer (b. 1900)
- July 19 – Harry Stockwell, American actor and singer (b. 1902)
- July 24 – Armando Morales Barillas, Nicaraguan guitarist (b. 1936)

- July 25 – Big Mama Thornton, American singer (b. 1926)
- July 26
    - George Gallup, American statistician and opinion pollster (b. 1901)
    - Ed Gein, American serial killer (b. 1906)
- July 27 – James Mason, British actor (b. 1909)
- July 28 – Bess Flowers, American actress (b. 1898)
- July 29 – Fred Waring, American bandleader (b. 1900)

August

Richard Burton

Truman Capote

- August 2 – Quirino Cristiani, Argentine animated film director (b. 1896)
- August 4 – Mary Miles Minter, American actress (b. 1902)
- August 5 – Richard Burton, Welsh actor (b. 1925)
- August 8 – Richard Deacon, American actor (b. 1921)
- August 11
    - Alfred A. Knopf, American publisher (b. 1892)

- o Paul Felix Schmidt, Estonian–German chess player (b. 1916)
- August 12 – Christine Hargreaves, English actress (b. 1939)
- August 13
    - o Clyde Cook, Australian actor (b. 1891)
    - o Tigran Petrosian, Georgian chess player (b. 1929)
- August 14 – J. B. Priestley, English novelist and playwright (b. 1894)
- August 25
    - o Truman Capote, American writer (b. 1924)
    - o Viktor Chukarin, Russian Olympic gymnast (b. 1921)
    - o Waite Hoyt, American baseball player (New York Yankees) and a member of the MLB Hall of Fame (b. 1899)
- August 27 – Bernard Youens, English actor (b. 1914)
- August 29 – Muhammad Naguib, 1st President of Egypt (b. 1901)

September

Janet Gaynor

- September 5
  - Adam Malik, 3rd Vice President of Indonesia (b. 1917)
  - Jane Roberts, American writer (b. 1929)
- September 6 – Ernest Tubb, American singer (b. 1914)
- September 7 – Joe Cronin, American baseball player (Boston Red Sox) and a member of the MLB Hall of Fame (b. 1906)
- September 8 – Frank Lowson English Test Cricketer 1951–1955 (b.1925)
- September 9 – Yılmaz Güney Turkish film director (b.1937)
- September 10 – Ismael Merlo, Spanish actor (b. 1918)
- September 14
  - Richard Brautigan, American counter-culture author (suicide) (b. 1935)
  - Janet Gaynor, American Academy Award-winning actress (b. 1906)
- September 17 – Richard Basehart, American actor (b. 1914)
- September 20 – Steve Goodman, American folk musician and songwriter (b. 1948)
- September 24 – Neil Hamilton, American actor (b. 1899)
- September 25 – Walter Pidgeon, Canadian actor (b. 1897)
- September 27 – Toke Townley, English actor (b. 1912)

October

Paul Dirac

Indira Gandhi

- October 1 – Walter Alston, American baseball player and manager (Brooklyn and Los Angeles Dodgers) and a member of the MLB Hall of Fame (b. 1911)
- October 5 – Leonard Rossiter, British actor (b. 1926)
- October 6 – George Gaylord Simpson, American paleontologist (b. 1902)
- October 12 – Sir Anthony Berry, British politician (bombing) (b. 1925)

- October 13 – George Kelly, American baseball player (New York Giants) and a member of the MLB Hall of Fame (b. 1895)
- October 14 – Martin Ryle, English radio astronomer, recipient of the Nobel Prize in Physics (b. 1918)
- October 16 – Peggy Ann Garner, American actress (b. 1932)
- October 18 – Jon-Erik Hexum, American actor (b. 1957)
- October 19 – Henri Michaux, Belgian writer and painter (b. 1899)
- October 20
    - Carl Ferdinand Cori, Austrian-born biochemist, recipient of the Nobel Prize in Physiology or Medicine (b. 1896)
    - Paul Dirac, English physicist, Nobel Prize laureate (b. 1902)
- October 21 – François Truffaut, French film director (b. 1932)
- October 23
    - David Gorcey, American actor (b. 1921)
    - Oskar Werner, Austrian actor (b. 1922)
- October 24 – Walter Woolf King, American singer and actor (b. 1899)
- October 30 – June Duprez, English actress (b. 1918)
- October 31
    - Eduardo De Filippo, Italian actor (b. 1900)
    - Indira Gandhi, Prime Minister of India (assassinated) (b. 1917)

November

- November 6 – Gastón Suárez, Bolivian novelist and dramatist (b. 1929)
- November 14 – Cesar Climaco, Filipino politician (assassinated) (b. 1916)
- November 16
    - Vic Dickenson, American trombonist (b. 1906)
    - Leonard Rose, American cellist (leukemia) (b. 1918)
- November 18 – Mary Hamman, American writer and editor, modern living editor *LIFE* and editor in chief *Bride & Home* (b. 1907)

December

Peter Lawford

- December 1 – Roelof Frankot, Dutch painter (b. 1911)
- December 4 – Jack Mercer, Voice of Popeye the Sailor (b. 1910)
- December 5 – Cecil M. Harden, American politician (b. 1894)
- December 8
    - Luther Adler, American actor (b. 1903)

- o Razzle, English drummer (Hanoi Rocks) (b. 1960)
- o Robert Jay Mathews, leader of the neo-Nazi terrorist group The Order
- December 11
  - o Oskar Seidlin, Silesian-born Jewish-American literary scholar (b. 1911)
  - o George Waggner, American film director (b. 1894)
- December 14 – Vicente Aleixandre, Spanish writer, Nobel Prize laureate (b. 1898)
- December 15 – Jan Peerce, American tenor (b. 1904)
- December 16
  - o Karl Deichgräber, German classical philologist (b. 1903)
  - o J. Roderick MacArthur, American businessman and philanthropist (b. 1920)
- December 20
  - o Gonzalo Márquez, Venezuelan Major League Baseball player (b. 1946)
  - o Dmitriy Ustinov, Soviet Army officer and Minister of Defense (b. 1908)
  - o Stanley Milgram, American psychologist (b. 1933)
- December 24 – Peter Lawford, English actor (b. 1923)
- December 28 – Sam Peckinpah, American film director (b. 1925)
- December 29 – Leo Robin, American composer (b. 1900)

Nobel Prizes

- Physics – Carlo Rubbia, Simon van der Meer
- Chemistry – Robert Bruce Merrifield
- Medicine – Niels Kaj Jerne, Georges J. F. Köhler, César Milstein
- Literature – Jaroslav Seifert
- Peace – Bishop Desmond Mpilo Tutu
- Bank of Sweden Prize in Economic Sciences in Memory of Alfred Nobel – Richard Stone

1984 in fiction

- The novel *Nineteen Eighty-Four* by George Orwell, published in 1949, is set in this year.
- The video game *Grand Theft Auto: Vice City Stories* takes place in 1984.
- *Metal Gear Solid V: The Phantom Pain* takes place in this year.
- *The Terminator* takes place in May of this year.
- *The Breakfast Club* Saturday school detention takes place on 24 March 1984

In the news.

Indian Prime minister Indira Gandhi assassinated.

The Olympic Games are held in Los Angeles.

WPC Yvonne Fletcher a London police officer is shot and killed by Libyan Diplomat.

English pound notes are to be taken out of circulation.

IRA Bomb goes off in Grand Hotel Brighton during Conservative Conference.

The Winter Olympic Games are held in Sarajevo, Yugoslavia.

Aids Virus identified by French Immunologist.

The first Apple Macintosh goes on sale.

Sony and Philips introduce the first commercial CD Players.

During November of 1984, 44 group members of "Band Aid" came together to record the single "Do They Know It's Christmas?" in a London studio.

Michael Jackson wins unprecedented acclaim for his Album Thriller and sales over 37 million copies.

Popular Films – Ghostbusters, Indiana Jones and the Temple of Doom, Gremlins, Beverly Hills Cop, Terms of Endearment, The Karate Kid, Star Trek III: The Search for Spock, Police Academy,

Romancing the Stone, Splash, The Terminator, Amadeus, The
Killing Fields, A Passage To India.

Popular TV Programmes - Magnum, P.I. Dynasty, Entertainment
Tonight, Falcon Crest, Hill Street Blues, Cagney and Lacey,
Cheers, Fame, Knight Rider, The A-Team, Jeopardy!

1984 Calendar

January 1984
Sun	Mon	Tue	Wed	Thu	Fri	Sat
1	2	3	4	5	6	7
8	9	10	11	12	13	14
15	16	17	18	19	20	21
22	23	24	25	26	27	28
29	30	31				

February 1984
Sun	Mon	Tue	Wed	Thu	Fri	Sat
			1	2	3	4
5	6	7	8	9	10	11
12	13	14	15	16	17	18
19	20	21	22	23	24	25
26	27	28	29			

March 1984
Sun	Mon	Tue	Wed	Thu	Fri	Sat
				1	2	3
4	5	6	7	8	9	10
11	12	13	14	15	16	17
18	19	20	21	22	23	24
25	26	27	28	29	30	31

April 1984
Sun	Mon	Tue	Wed	Thu	Fri	Sat
1	2	3	4	5	6	7
8	9	10	11	12	13	14
15	16	17	18	19	20	21
22	23	24	25	26	27	28
29	30					

May 1984
Sun	Mon	Tue	Wed	Thu	Fri	Sat
		1	2	3	4	5
6	7	8	9	10	11	12
13	14	15	16	17	18	19
20	21	22	23	24	25	26
27	28	29	30	31		

June 1984
Sun	Mon	Tue	Wed	Thu	Fri	Sat
					1	2
3	4	5	6	7	8	9
10	11	12	13	14	15	16
17	18	19	20	21	22	23
24	25	26	27	28	29	30

July 1984
Sun	Mon	Tue	Wed	Thu	Fri	Sat
1	2	3	4	5	6	7
8	9	10	11	12	13	14
15	16	17	18	19	20	21
22	23	24	25	26	27	28
29	30	31				

August 1984
Sun	Mon	Tue	Wed	Thu	Fri	Sat
			1	2	3	4
5	6	7	8	9	10	11
12	13	14	15	16	17	18
19	20	21	22	23	24	25
26	27	28	29	30	31	

September 1984
Sun	Mon	Tue	Wed	Thu	Fri	Sat
						1
2	3	4	5	6	7	8
9	10	11	12	13	14	15
16	17	18	19	20	21	22
23	24	25	26	27	28	29
30						

October 1984
Sun	Mon	Tue	Wed	Thu	Fri	Sat
	1	2	3	4	5	6
7	8	9	10	11	12	13
14	15	16	17	18	19	20
21	22	23	24	25	26	27
28	29	30	31			

November 1984
Sun	Mon	Tue	Wed	Thu	Fri	Sat
				1	2	3
4	5	6	7	8	9	10
11	12	13	14	15	16	17
18	19	20	21	22	23	24
25	26	27	28	29	30	

December 1984
Sun	Mon	Tue	Wed	Thu	Fri	Sat
						1
2	3	4	5	6	7	8
9	10	11	12	13	14	15
16	17	18	19	20	21	22
23	24	25	26	27	28	29
30	31